W9-CGW-255

A Robbie Reader

Alex Rodriguez
PROFESSIONAL BASEBALL PLAYER

Marylou Morano Kjelle

P.O. Box 196
Hockessin, Delaware 19707
Visit us on the web: www.mitchelllane.com
Comments? email us: mitchelllane@mitchelllane.com

Mitchell Lane
PUBLISHERS

Printing   2   3   4   5   6   7   8

A Robbie Reader

Albert Einstein	**Alex Rodriguez**	Brittany Murphy
Charles Schulz	Dakota Fanning	Dale Earnhardt Jr.
Donovan McNabb	Dr. Seuss	Henry Ford
Hilary Duff	Jamie Lynn Spears	Jessie McCartney
Johnny Gruelle	LeBron James	Mia Hamm
Philo T. Farnsworth	Robert Goddard	Shaquille O'Neal
Shawna Robinson	The Story of Harley-Davidson	Syd Hoff
Thomas Edison	Tiki Barber	Tony Hawk

Library of Congress Cataloging-in-Publication Data
Kjelle, Marylou Morano.
    Alex Rodriguez / by Marylou Morano Kjelle.
       p. cm. — (A Robbie reader)
    Includes bibliographical references and index.
    ISBN 1-58415-394-6 (library bound)
    1. Rodriguez, Alex, 1975—Juvenile literature. 2. Baseball players—United States—Biography—Juvenile literature. I. Title. II. Series.
GV865.R62K54 2005
796.357'092—dc22
                             2005009731

ISBN-10: 1-58415-394-6   ISBN-13: 978-1-58415-394-8

ABOUT THE AUTHOR: Marylou Morano Kjelle is a freelance writer and photo-journalist who lives and works in central New Jersey. She is a regular contributor to several local newspaper and online publications. Marylou writes a column for the Westfield Leader/Times of Scotch Plains-Fanwood called "Children's Book Nook," where she reviews children's books. She has written fourteen nonfiction books for young readers and co-authored and edited others. Other titles she has written for Mitchell Lane are *Hilary Duff* and *Tony Hawk*. Marylou has a M.S. degree in Science from Rutgers University and teaches both science and writing at a community college in New Jersey.

PHOTO CREDITS: Cover—Ezra Shaw/Getty Images; p. 4—Gregory Bull/AP Photo; pp. 6, 8, 22—Sean Doughtery; pp. 9, 28—Jim McIsaac/Getty Images; p. 10—Jed Jacobsohn; p. 12—Pat Sullivan/AP Photo; p. 14—Jeffrey Boan/AP Photo; p. 16—Mitch Haddad/WireImage; p. 17—David Bergman/Corbis; pp. 18, 23—Jonathan Daniel/Allsport/Getty Images; p. 20—LM Otero/AP Photo; pp. 24, 27 (top)—Alexander Tamargo/Getty Images; p. 27 (bottom)—Marta Lavandier/AP Photo.
ACKNOWLEDGMENTS: The following story has been thoroughly researched, and to the best of our knowledge, represents a true story. While every possible effort has been made to ensure accuracy, the publisher will not assume liability for damages caused by inaccuracies in the data, and makes no warranty on the accuracy of the information contained herein. This story has not been authorized nor endorsed by anyone associated with Alex Rodriguez.

TABLE OF CONTENTS

Alex Rodriguez (center) buttons up his new #13 jersey during a news conference at Yankee Stadium. His manager, Joe Torres (left), and teammate, Derek Jeter (right), welcome him as a new member of the New York Yankees.

A-Rod Becomes a Yankee

On February 17, 2004, an **announcement (uh-NOUN-sment)** stunned the baseball world. Alex Rodriguez was leaving the Texas Rangers. "A-Rod," as he is called, was joining the New York Yankees.

Alex had played with the Texas Rangers for three years. He was team captain. He had won many awards and broken many records. In 2003 he was named the American **League's (LEEGS)** Most Valuable Player (MVP). But Alex wanted to play in the World Series. The Rangers finished last in the American League's West Division all three years. As a Yankee, he believed that he could lead his team into the World Series.

Alex Rodriguez steps up to bat shortly after he joined the New York Yankees in 2004.

"Winning is the most important thing to me," Alex told reporter Mark Feinsand in an interview after joining the Yankees.

Yankee fans were happy to have Alex on their team. A big sign outside Yankee Stadium said "A-Rod, Welcome to New York."

Winning a World Series **championship (CHAM-pee-un-ship)** was so important to Alex that he was willing to change his playing positions. He had always played shortstop, the infield position between second base and third base. But the Yankees had one of the best shortstops in the major leagues, Derek Jeter. Alex agreed to play third base.

Alex's first season with the Yankees ended in disappointment. The Boston Red Sox defeated the Yankees in the 2004 American League Championship Series. Then the Red Sox defeated the St. Louis Cardinals to win the World Series.

The Yankees are one of the best teams in Major League Baseball. There's a good chance that Alex will reach his goal yet.

Alex Rodriguez had always played shortstop, but when he joined the Yankees he changed his playing position because the team had Derek Jeter, one of the best shortstops in the major leagues. Here are Alex and Derek having a talk during a game.

Alex makes the catch on a pop-up.

Alex celebrates as he scores from third base on a home run.

The Son of Immigrants

Alex Emmanuel Rodriguez was born in New York City on July 27, 1975. His parents, **Lourdes (LOORD)** and Victor, came from the **Dominican Republic (doe-MIN-uh-kan ree-PUB-lik).** The Dominican Republic shares the Caribbean island of **Hispaniola (his-pan-YO-luh)** with the country of Haiti. Victor and Lourdes moved to the United States before Alex was born. They lived in an area of New York City called Washington Heights. Many of their neighbors were from the Dominican Republic. They all spoke Spanish.

Victor and Lourdes planned to work hard, save their money, and return to their native

Alex Rodriguez, short-stop, was the top pick in the June amateur draft for the 1993 U.S. Olympic Competition. Even before he made it into the Major Leagues, Alex was always willing to give advice to a young player.

country. Victor bought a shoe store and Lourdes worked in a factory that made cars. Alex had an older sister, Susy, and an older brother, Joe.

When Alex was four years old, his family returned to the Dominican Republic. They settled in the capital, Santo Domingo, and opened a business. The family lived in a big home near the beach. Alex's father had played baseball for a Dominican team. He taught Alex the game.

For a few years, life was good. Then the business failed. Victor and Lourdes had to sell their home. The family came back to the United States. They lived near Miami, Florida. Soon afterward, Victor left the family. He and Alex did not speak for many years.

Life was hard for Alex and his family. Lourdes worked two jobs to buy food and pay the rent. Alex was shy. He had to learn to speak English. Alex was angry at his father for leaving.

Alex Rodriguez, a senior shortstop at Westminster Christian Academy High School in Miami, Florida, was named the 1993 National High School Baseball Player of the Year by the Gatorade Company.

Becoming the Best

To take his mind off his troubles, Alex played baseball. One of his coaches, Juan Diego Arteaga, became like a second father to Alex.

Juan Diego's son, J.D., became Alex's best friend. The boys joined the Hank Kline Boys Club in Miami. They played on the club's baseball team. A man named Eddy Rodriguez (no relation) was the coach. Some of Eddy's players had made it into the major leagues. Eddy told Alex he was good enough to play in the major leagues, too.

Alex played shortstop. Another shortstop, Cal Ripken, Jr., of the Baltimore Orioles, was Alex's hero. Alex hung a life-size poster of Ripken over his bed.

Alex and J.D. both went to Westminster Christian Academy High School. They were on the football team. In 1990, Juan Diego collapsed during the season's first game. He died later that day. Alex lost his second father.

Alex studied hard and made the honor roll. He planned to go to college. But his baseball coach, Rich Hofman, told Alex he could be the best high school baseball player in the United States.

"Work hard this year," Coach Hofman told Alex when he was in eleventh grade.

From the time he was a youngster, Alex Rodriguez has been a huge fan of Cal Ripken. In 2001, Alex played in the All Star Game with his boyhood baseball hero.

The hard work paid off. In 1992, the Westminster Warriors were the top-ranked high school baseball team in the country. That summer, Alex played shortstop for the United States team at the World Junior Championships in Mexico. The team placed second.

Alex graduated from high school in 1993 with a .419 **batting average**. He was six feet three inches and 195 pounds of pure baseball power. He was about to prove that Coach Hofman was right.

Alex attended Westminster Christian Academy High School. He became a member of the baseball team, the Westminster Warriors.

In 1993, Alex was the first player selected in the Major League Baseball Draft. He was drafted by the Seattle Mariners and played with the Mariners for six years before signing with the Texas Rangers.

Superstar Shortstop

Alex was the first player chosen in the 1993 Major League Baseball Draft. He was **drafted** by the Seattle Mariners. Alex was also offered a baseball **scholarship (SKAW-lur-ship)** by the University of Miami. The school wanted him to play on their team, the Hurricanes.

At first, Alex turned down the Seattle Mariners. Then they offered him more than a million dollars. It was a lot of money for someone who had just turned eighteen. Alex accepted the offer. He made a promise to his mother. Someday he would go to college. But for now he would play baseball.

Alex Rodriguez of the Seattle Mariners jumps off second base trying to avoid Texas Rangers Mark McLemore as he slides to the base.

For the first two years, Alex played part of the season in the **minor leagues**. He also played in some games with the Mariners.

In 1996, he played the entire season with the Mariners. He won the American League batting title with a .358 batting average. *Sporting News*, a newspaper that covers baseball, gave Alex their Major League Player of the Year award.

Alex stayed with Seattle for six years. In 2000, he became a **free agent**. Now he could play for any team. The Texas Rangers offered him a ten-year contract and $252 million dollars. The contract made history. No other baseball player had been offered so much money. Some people thought it was too much to pay a ballplayer. Alex was called **greedy (GREE-dee)**. Seattle Mariner fans booed him on the field.

"[Money] doesn't make you who you are," Alex told Alan Schwarz of *Sports Illustrated for Kids*. "I still see myself as just a baseball player."

Alex signed a contract with the Texas Rangers in the year 2000 and became the highest paid baseball player in history at that time.

Alex Gonzalez of the Chicago Cubs attempts to tag Alex Rodriguez "out," but Rodriguez is safe as he slides into second base.

Alex married Cynthia Scurtis in November of 2002. They have a baby daughter, Natasha, who was born in 2004.

CHAPTER FIVE

A Solid Citizen

There is more to Alex than baseball. On November 2, 2002, he married Cynthia Scurtis. She was a high school **psychology (sy-KALL-oh-gee)** teacher. Both are people of strong faith. In November 2004, their daughter, Natasha, was born.

Off the baseball field, Alex loves to read and play golf. He visits schools to tell children not to drink, use drugs, or smoke. In the off-season, Alex studies at the University of Miami. He is taking business courses to fulfill the promise he made to his mother. He told her he would get a college degree.

In 1996, he started a program called "Grand Slam for Kids." It helps children become better at math, reading, physical fitness, and good citizenship. To Alex, these are life's "four bases."

Two years later, he established the Alex Rodriguez Foundation. The clubs teach children to care for their community as well as themselves. The Foundation also gave money to victims of Hurricane George in the Dominican Republic.

In 2002, Alex gave nearly four million dollars to the University of Miami. The money was used to rebuild the school's baseball stadium. It is called Alex Rodriguez Park.

Alex has not forgotten his roots. He is a national **spokesperson** for the Boys and Girls Clubs of America. He has given money to the club in Miami where he and J.D. played ball as boys.

On June 8, 2005, Alex became the youngest player ever to hit 400 home runs in his career. On the field or off, Alex Rodriguez is a winner.

Alex and his wife Cynthia donated $500,000 to the Boys and Girls Club of Miami. Alex is the national spokesperson for the club.

Alex donated $3.9 million dollars to rebuild University of Miami's baseball stadium and to fund a scholarship for a Boys and Girls Club member. In his honor the stadium is named Alex Rodriguez Park.

Alex Rodriguez is six feet three inches and 195 pounds of pure baseball power.

BATTING STATISTICS

Year	Team	G	AB	R	H	2B	3B	HR	RBI	AVG
1994	SEA	17	54	4	11	0	0	0	2	.204
1995	SEA	28	142	15	33	6	2	5	19	.232
1996	SEA	146	601	141	215	54	1	36	123	.358
1997	SEA	141	587	100	176	40	3	23	84	.300
1998	SEA	161	686	123	213	35	5	42	124	.310
1999	SEA	129	502	110	143	25	0	42	111	.285
2000	SEA	148	554	134	175	34	2	41	132	.316
2001	TEX	162	632	133	201	34	1	52	135	.318
2002	TEX	162	624	125	187	27	2	57	142	.300
2003	TEX	161	607	124	181	30	6	47	118	.298
2004	NYY	155	601	112	172	24	2	36	106	.286
2005	NYY	162	605	124	194	29	1	48	130	.321

1975 Alex Rodriguez was born on July 27

1992 Alex's team, the Westminster Warriors, is the top-ranked high school baseball team in the country; he plays in the World Junior Championships in Mexico

1993 Alex is the first player selected in the Major League Baseball Draft

1996 Alex plays his first full major league season with the Seattle Mariners and has the highest batting average in the American League

1998 Alex becomes the third player in baseball history to join the "40-40 club" (He hits 40 home runs and steals 40 bases in one season)

2000 Alex joins the Texas Rangers and becomes the highest paid player in baseball history

2001 Alex plays in the All Star Game with his boyhood baseball hero, Cal Ripken, Jr.

2002 Alex wins the Golden Glove Award as the best-fielding American League shortstop and is named Major League Player of the Year for the second time by *Sporting News*; he marries Cynthia Scurtis

2003 Alex wins the American League Most Valuable Player award

2004 Alex joins the New York Yankees; his daughter Natasha is born

2005 Alex saves Patrick McCarthy from being hit by a truck; he becomes the youngest player in baseball to hit 400 home runs in his career

announcement (uh-NOUN-sment)—a public notice.

batting average (BAT-ting AV-er-ehj)—total base hits divided by the number of times at bat.

championship (CHAM-pee-un-ship)—a contest to determine a winner of first prize or first place in a competition.

draft—system for selecting people.

free agent—person who is no longer under contract with an organization.

greedy (GREE-dee)—wanting a lot of money or things.

minor leagues (myner LEEGS)—the lower levels of professional baseball.

psychology (sy-KALL-oh-gee)—the study of human behavior.

scholarship (SKAW-lur-ship)—money given to pay for school or college.

spokesperson (SPOHKS-per-son)—someone who tells the public about an organization.

Armentrout, David and Patricia Armentrout. *Alex Rodriguez.* Vero Beach, Florida: Rourke Publishing, 2003.

Bradley, Michael. *Alex Rodriguez.* Tarrytown, New York: Benchmark Books, 2004.

Christensen, Joe. *Alex Rodriguez.* Edina, Minnesota: Checkerboard Books, 2003.

Covert, Kim. *Alex Rodriguez.* Mankato, Minnesota: Capstone High Interest Books, 2002.

Rappoport, Ken. *Super Sports Star Alex Rodriguez.* Berkeley Heights, New Jersey: Enslow Publishers, 2004.

Rodriguez, Alex. *Hit a Grand Slam.* Dallas: Taylor Publishing Company, 1998.

Stewart, Mark. *Alex Rodriguez: Gunning for Greatness.* Brookfield, Connecticut: Millbrook Press, 1999.

Zuehlke, Jeffrey. *Alex Rodriguez.* Minneapolis, Minnesota: LernerSports, 2005.

WEBSITES
Official Site of the New York Yankees
http://newyork.yankees.mlb.com
Alex Rodriguez statistics and awards
http://www.baseball-reference.com/r/rodrial01.shtml
Sports Illustrated Alex Rodriguez page
http://sportsillustrated.cnn.com/baseball/mlb/players/5275/

INDEX